PROSPERITY COMMANDMENTS

Rev. Dr. Della Reese Lett

Lett/Reese International Publishing Company

Production Manager: Wally White

Production Coordinator: Jodi Smith

Cover Photograph: Cliff Lipson

Cover Design: Franklin Lett

Cover Graphic Design and Layout: Sean Stearley

PROSPERITY COMMANDMENTS

THIS PAGE INTENTIONALLY LEFT BLANK

PREFACE

My mother was and really still is my hero although she left this planet in 1949. She was my hero and the wind beneath my wings. She gave me what was necessary to rise up and out of the slums of Detroit, Michigan.

Because of her beliefs, attitudes and understanding of God she had a personal relationship with God. I have had a relationship with God all my life; my mother required it. She used her relationship to feed us sometimes, heal us sometimes and although there were few luxuries, there was great love and peace of mind.

Leaving home for my chosen career when I was seventeen, after my mother died all I had was my talent and the understandings my mother had taught me; engrained in me is more like it. They are responsible for my being able to work in the world and not be of it.

One day thirty-two years ago I walked into a church in Chicago, Illinois and heard a woman expressing the thoughts my mother had taught me. She was using different words but the meanings were the same. Positive faith and the witnessing to the actual use of prayer and faith for living in a better way here and now!

I had to know her, and I am proud to say I have that privilege. Reverend Dr. Johnnie Colemon is "My Buddy" and through her teaching I gained a metaphysical understanding. She taught me how to see my REAL SELF, the one Jesus Christ came to teach us about, the self that is made in the image likeness of God.

The self, filled with the power of God placed inside of me, so that I (we) may have life and that more abundantly, through understanding, prayer, meditation and faith.

Dr. Colemon of course introduced me to many branches of knowledge. I have had the privilege to study the works of Reverend Dr. Colemon, Charles Fillmore, George Lamsa, H. Emilie Cady, Catherine Ponder, Rocco Errico, Joseph Murphy, Robert A. Russell, Elizabeth Sand Turner, Jack Ensign Addington, Georgiana Tree West and Joel S. Goldsmith to name a few.

Since God is the Truth, has always been the Truth, and God never changes, this is by no means a new TRUTH. For there is no new Truth, and no DIFFERENT TRUTH, only God and more God unchanging. There are many things in this book you have heard or seen or even thought about on your own. This is just the way I have taught these lessons and seen the benefits to the lives of my congregation, and I would like to share them. I believe with Jesus, "Whosoever will, let him come."

Let him come, and "study, show thyself approved unto God, a workman that needs not to be ashamed rightly dividing the word of truth." 2 Timothy 2:15

The lessons in this book are transcribed from live sermons I have given at Understanding Principles for Better Living Church in Los Angeles, CA. I have a way of pausing to give my listeners a moment to think or question themselves. I stop, say "Huh," and then continue. When you see that throughout this book, I invite you to take those same moments to think and question yourself.

Rev. Della

THE GREAT COMMANDMENT

"Thou shalt love the Lord Thy God with all thy heart and all thy soul and with all thy mind."　　　　　Mark 12:30

This is it; make no mistake, with all your heart. The heart, metaphysically, is your subconscious mind. That is where you store that trash that hinders your having a more abundant life. You have to love God with all of that, so the trash can be disintegrated. Love Him with all your heart, your soul, which is all your feelings. Your feelings are your actions, your reactions and emotions.

Some of you only give Him your feelings in church on Sunday mornings. When the music is good or when you are in dire trouble or grief. You talk the talk, but you never walk the walk. There is a scripture where Jesus says, "I spit you out of my mouth because you are neither hot nor cold!" He would spit out a lot of people reading this lesson. Why? Because, your feelings for God are so "sometimey". If God is good you should say so, act so and be grateful in the glory of that goodness. And if you do not like it, quit conning yourself and anybody else that will buy into it and say so.

"For God so loved the world He gave His only begotten son, that whosoever believed in Him should not perish, but have everlasting life."　　　　　John 3:16

Notice it did not say the chosen few. It does not say the African-American. It does not say the Presbyterian. It does not say the Baptist or the New Thought Christian nor the Chinese. It says, "whosoever." That is anybody who will believe God's love is a gift to us. God gave, He so loved the world, He gave. It is not love until you give it away. The way to love is to give it away. Love is deeper than we give it credit for being. Yes, it is passion and passionate but more than that, love is God!

Here are His instructions:

"And word of the Lord God come unto Zechariah saying, thus speaks the Lord of host saying, execute true judgment and show mercy and compassions every man to his brother: and let none of you imagine evil against his brother in your heart."   Zechariah 7:8-9-10

You don't know why I did whatever it was I did, so don't go imagining. You have been in that set of circumstances. You have assumed something, only to find out later what you imagined was not the way it was going at all. Huh? What kept you motivated along the train of thought you took were those dirty pictures in your mind. Someone just thought, *"Well, what else would you do in a place like that... in a case like that?"* They were both in there; they must have been doing something!

Jesus talking, *"What matter that to thee, you follow Me."* Of course they were doing something, but not necessarily the little something you were thinking and talking about. Do not imagine evil against your brother in your heart.

"Thou shall love thy neighbor as thy self love your enemies, bless them that curse you. Do good to them that hate you."   Matthew 5:44

Someone thought "ridiculous." While you are trying to love your enemy, he is stabbing you in the back. If you really want to set a sucker crazy and he is your enemy, HUG that sucker and say, *"God Bless you today. God bless you today. I want today to be for you everything you want it to be, and everything God wants it to be. If you need any help, you just call me";* and mean it! It's never about them, it is always about you. I love this, *"He that loves, fulfills the law."* Get this: *"Owe no man anything but to love one another."*   Romans 13:8

Hear me good now, real good. Whatever is happening in my life, I drew it to me. Good, bad, or indifferent. Now, you might have been the messenger that God gave it to bring it to me. Good, bad, or indifferent. But, had I not been consciously aware, you could not have given it to me. So, I don't owe you. Therefore I have no guilt about what you have done for me. You have done for me what I have projected into manifestation through you. Are you getting this at all? So don't come to me and tell me I ought to do anything because of what you have done for me.

THE GREAT COMMANDMENT

If I am going to do anything for you, it is out of my love for you, not out of your love for me or what you did for me. We are inter-wound in each other's lives. There is no guilt attached to it. Haven't you ever noticed you don't see people for ten years and at the moment you need this particular thing, they appear? You are here, designed to do certain things for me. I accept them, I am grateful. For I know what you did fills the notch that takes me to the next place. But I don't owe you anything. Whatever you did for me, God told you to do it 'cause I asked Him for it. If I love the Lord and my neighbor as myself, I know love should be without dissimulation. Dissimulation is to disguise something, to conceal it under false appearances; to conceal your true motives and thoughts, and pretend. Hypocrites dissimulate. Jesus says,

"Love... do this and you shall live."   Luke 10:28

"He that loves Me shall be loved by My Father."
     John 14:21

"And a new commandment I give to you; Love one another."   John 13:34

"He that loves his brother abides in the light."
     John 2:10

How many of you love the Lord? Are you aware that loving is something you do, not just something you say?

THE GREAT COMMANDMENT

Love is a verb and action word. *"If you love Me keep my commandments,"* John 14:15

Now you say you love the Lord. How do you treat GOD? I know He treats you accordingly to His nature, which is absolute good. But how do you treat GOD? Do you lie to Him and break your promises? Do you cheat Him out of the proper respect, attention and appreciation for the love He gives you? Do you rob Him? Do you take all the profits of your life and not give Him His share? Do you ignore Him until you need Him?

Since obedience is the spirit of love (because love is the most obedient thing in the Universe), it is the greatest worker and will accomplish more for our happiness than all the other faculties combined. Do you slap Him in the face with your constant disobedience of His word even though His love rules justly and righteously? His love defeats the destructiveness that would harm you, puts your affairs in order, and replaces opposition and fear with cooperation and trust.

Do you abuse Him with your anger, jealousy, fear, anxieties and disbelief? Even though He has told us that love vaunteth not itself (does not boast or brag, is not puffed up); do you insult Him with your attitudes of snobbishness and your lack of humbleness and your willingness to do anything for self-satisfaction?

THE GREAT COMMANDMENT

"If you ask anything in my name I will do it".

John 14:14

Do you disregard this, by complaining and bugging your friends and family with your distress stories? How can you say you love God when you treat Him that way? Yet no matter what, He takes care of you day and night, everyday and night in spite of how you treat Him. He deserves something larger, much more, a whole lot better. And so do you!

It is time for a different love relationship with God, a real love relationship with God. It is time for your life to be an action and not just a series of reactions. A real love relationship with God, using your faith and love, which are an electrical force, combined with the love that God has stored up for you. It will find you loving the life you live, and living the life you love.

I am love! I live by The Law of Love! Love is now and always will be victorious! I am the love of God in expression. I let God's love guide me, direct me, inspire me right now and forever more. God's love in me is drawing to me new ideas, new courage into visible daily supply. I am the prospering power of God's love. I am absolutely determined to treat God better than I have been. I am going to consciously show I have love and respect for my Father God and His Son Christ Jesus and the Holy Spirit. Because you love me Father, I walk in the charmed circle of Your love and am divinely irresistible to my highest good.

THE SECOND PROSPERITY COMMANDMENT

"Thou shall not make unto thee any graven image, or any likeness of anything that is in heaven above, or that is in the earth beneath or that is in the water under the earth."

Exodus 20:4

"Thou shall make no mental images of lack."

False beliefs: lack, limitation, sickness, pain, fear, anxiety, poverty – are all false beliefs. They occur, but they have only the power you give them. Since God is absolute good, if you are worshipping lack you have a graven image. Attitudes are graven images you have carved into the very fiber of your subconscious mind. Formulating and holding a belief is planting a seed. Law: *"As a man soweth, so shall he reap."* If you do not want it, do not sow it! The Law of Force is the second plane of supply. The Law of Force belongs to the carnivorous animals. They prey on lesser creatures.

There are human carnivorous animals. They are racketeers, robbers, grafters, extortionists, blackmailers, users, and parasites of all kinds. They operate by force, cunning, deception and by taking advantage. They prey on those who have. When we lower ourselves to a plane beneath the spiritual status we pay a terrible price – the loss of respect, our own and others; loss of peace of mind, loss of liberty and often loss of life itself, which is not always physical death. Loss of life is when you are not in control of your life. Because we are made in the image likeness of God, we have every plane of supply in us, including The Law of Force. We have to learn how to apply The Law of Force in and on the highest level, which is the spiritual level. This may be a new idea to some of you, that's all right. Force is a Law of Supply on the spiritual level. The contract says, *"The Kingdom of heaven suffereth violence and the violent take it by force,"*

Matthew 11:12

Not the force of the animal kingdom, not material force, but spiritual force. Most of you quit too soon. You surrender too soon to the apparent. That is why Jesus told us to judge not by appearances (the apparent). Most of the time all that is necessary is to assert yourself and you can turn the tide or walk the water if you have to, if you will judge the righteous judgment. Prosperity requires enduring persistence. You have to wrestle with fact and break through the struggle of appearances, by exercising the will of force in the matter of supply. I am not talking about physical will (outer results). It is exercising the inner will to the point of complete reliance on God, recognition and complete reliance on God, not only as a source, but the supply itself.

Faith is greater than will. Your will is only efficient when you use it to awaken or conform to faith. That is why the greatest prayer you can pray is, *"Not my will but thy will be done."* Because when you let go and let God, you get action. It is not by asserting your puny will (in comparison with God's will of absolute good), you invoke "The Law of Great Irresistible Force."

You then use your will to keep out of God's way, to keep your thoughts and actions God-like, no matter what the appearance. Your will is not your greatest asset, your faith is. Faith is your real wealth and your force that produces. In order to have great prosperity, you have got to produce and that more abundantly.

It takes courage to trust God. You must dare to trust God and have faith in Him as your instant, constant, manifested supply. Even when you cannot see it with your physical eye, you must use your spiritual eye (your faith). You must see it spiritually and you must hold to that picture no matter who, what, why, or whatever, with the power of force in your faith.

"Faith is the substance of things hoped for, the evidence of things not seen."   Hebrews 11:1

"If you have faith and do not doubt, nothing shall be impossible to you."   Matthew 17:20

"According to your faith, be it done unto you."

Matthew 9:29

Jesus trying to secure our strongest tool, prayed for us and His prayer, *"I have prayed for you that thy faith not fail."*

Luke 22:32

Of all the things He could have prayed for us, He prayed for what is our strongest force, our faith. Faith is an irresistible and all achieving force. Faith knows and knowledge is power, *"For you shall know the truth and the truth shall set you free."* Knowing is a magnet and it pulls into being that which it is attached to.

"Be of good comfort, thy faith hath made thee whole! Thy faith has saved thee, go in peace."

Matthew 9:22

When you thoroughly and deeply, really understand and accept these truths you are ready to invoke the Second Prosperity Commandment. *"Thou shall make no mental images of lack."*

I am talking about statues of golden cows and Egyptian heads of serpents and other animals. We make graven images and bow down to them and serve them. False beliefs are graven images.

Formulating and holding a belief is planting a seed either way, good or bad. It is creative thought power. Our minds are creative thought in action.

Have you ever heard the expression, "Train of thought"? Train: a vehicle that delivers something to a certain destination. Train of thought: a vehicle that delivers its creative power into manifestation.

Thinking is the first plane of supply because thinking is the formative process of your mind. It is the inlet and outlet of your ideas. It is your creative center.

When you send or direct your creative power to lack in any form, you create a poverty station. Then you fill it with fearful, unhappy, sordid beliefs. You bow down to them and serve them. What are you talking about Rev. Della? You tell yourself you can't handle whatever the situation is ~ which is a lie. Then you give yourself reasons to make this lie correct. And with your gut feelings you bow down to the lie and serve it. By doing this, all other thought is paralyzed.

Have you ever been asked for advice and you give it with good caring faith, with truthful information, and the person listens until you are finished and they say, *"I know that but you really don't understand"* or *"That's easy for you to say"*?

Their thoughts are paralyzed by the thought that is their graven image. They never heard you once they knew you would not worship their image also. *"As a man thinks in his heart so is he,"* that is in the Old Testament. The New Testament says, *"like produces like."* In Genesis, God instructs us that, *"things produce after their own kind."*

Jesus said, *"The good man out of his good treasure brings forth good, and the evil man out of his evil treasure brings forth evil."* Appearances are evidences of the senses. Sometimes our conditions or conditioning of our physical side make appearances difficult to repudiate. Enter The Law of Force. You must whip the appearance down, wrestle it down and whip it into shape. If you have to — punch it out! We, like the prodigal son, have to come out of "the far country." Out of that realm of mind that is so far from God. You cannot afford to get hung up with the people of "the far country." The people of the far country are lack, limitation, sickness, pain, fear, anxiety, poverty; and are all fed by false beliefs. If you do, you will find yourself feeding the swine, drudging for mere physical existence in a very ignoble manner.

We must return to our Father's house. We must come to ourselves. We must remember who, what, and whose we are. No matter what we must know the truth, for the truth is what sets us free. *"What is this truth,"* someone may be asking. The truth is, *"There is only one power and one presence in the Universe, and that power is God, the*

Good. Omnipotent, omniscient and omnipresent. He is the Father that loves me and His will for me is absolute good." Jesus talking, *"Verily I say unto you, whosoever shall say onto this mountain, be thou removed and be thou cast into the sea, and shall not doubt in his heart, but shall believe in that those things which he says come to pass; he shall have whatsoever he says. Therefore I say unto you what things so ever you desire, when you pray believe that you receive them and you shall have them.*

Mark 11:23-24

If you abide in Me, and My words abide in you, you shall ask what you will and it shall be done unto you".

John 15:7

The thoughts you have been thinking and the appearances you have been bowing down to are responsible for what is happening in your life right now. Remember, that what you acknowledge to be your master... to that, you are a servant.

THE THIRD PROSPERITY COMMANDMENT

"Thou shall not speak the word of lack or limitation."

The Arabic root word for vain is <u>*Da-Fa-Looth*</u> and it means falsehood. *"You shall not take the name of the Lord, your God, falsely! For He will not hold you guiltless if you do."* Exodus 20:7

Exodus 3:13-15 tells us God's name, *"I AM"* and how we know His name and that His name will remain the same forever, and that this is God's memorial unto all generations. *"I AM"* is your true identity. These are the only two words in the vocabulary that no one else can speak for you, but you.

Stay with me now,

"So shall my word be that goes forth out of my mouth: It shall not return to me void; but it shall accomplish that which I please, and it shall prosper in the thing where I send it." Isaiah 55:11

"But I say unto you, that every idle word that men shall speak, they shall give account therefore in the day of judgment. For by thy words thou shall be justified and by thou words shalt be condemned." Matthew 12:36-37

THE THIRD PROSPERITY COMMANDMENT

God's gift to us is Power, Dominion, Mastery, and His Authority to use these "forces" over all created things. Our bodies, minds, our worlds and affairs are created things. We contact this power with our words as our Father did. There is in each of us a "Little Me" and a "Great Me." The "Little Me" reacts in anger, seeks revenge, criticizes, complains, takes God's name in vain, lies generally and on God in particular. The "Great Me" expects to receive, is prepared to receive. The "Little Me" is always saying *"I am so sick! In the name of God, I want to be so sick. I am so tired, I am never gonna get out of this mess no matter what I decide. I am always wrong."* In the name of God, make me tired, sick and never let me decide what is right so I can get out of this mess. This is breaking the Third Commandment and the Third Prosperity Law. You know what happens when you break The Law? A: Punishment by The Law.

Your "Great Me", the "Spiritually Inspired Me", works in the awareness of the divine flow of power, intelligence and creativity that is its divine inheritance. There is power in the words you speak. So when you speak of lack and limitation, you give it power. Your "Great Me," speaks words of abundance because it knows it is God's divine design for us to be abundant. When you do this, your friends and neighbors who mostly live in their "Little Me" will think you are conceited, you are NOT. You are confident in your faith in God.

Here enters the third plane of Prosperity: Work. You have to work at it because you have been speaking words of lack and limitation so long, it has become natural and normal in your daily conversation. You must speak words of abundance in order to overcome all the lack and limitation in your life.

Then comes the hard part. You must work at believing what you say. There are laws of compensation and balance. *"Whatever measure you mete, shall be measured again unto you."* Sooner or later, depending on our faith, The Law of Balance must work for you.

EXAMPLE: Salary is compensation for services rendered; that is balance. In order to get ahead, you must get ahead of The Law and give more than you receive. When you are dealing with The Law, not only do you receive more, but new opportunities work to get you greater returns. They present themselves to you, specifically designed for you. Progress is the result of being in tune with The Law. Voluntary giving of your very best takes the place of an exacted toll then your returns voluntarily increase. Things will change. Before now you were trying to find and get. When you work with The Law, what you want seeks and finds you. I am not talking about physical work. Physical work is only a means of outward expression.

It is a muscle, not a character builder. Your mind working behind your muscles builds skill. Drudgery leaves the work, and you begin to work for the purpose of expressing, developing and perfecting your skills. Then you use work as a means of growth and expansion. Your spiritual work is to *"Seek ye first the Kingdom of Heaven and all these things shall be added unto you."*

You need to pray without ceasing and to meditate upon the work of the Lord and to affirm it. This builds your inner sense of wealth. You have to build attitudes and motives that govern the outer.

EXAMPLE: I expect and will accept no compensation. I am doing this as a gift. It is my pleasure. Mental and spiritual work is first achieving power in the inner. You've got to feel it. You've got to feel the riches of your true state, your spiritual inheritance. You have to work on it until you feel it and pray until you are so filled that even the outer seeming poverty you are experiencing at this moment cannot impress you at all. Remember when you pray, prayer is an attitude not a platitude. You are not begging. Did you hear me? You are not begging you are obeying.

God told us to ask Him, and asking is claiming what is rightfully yours. Prayer is your communication with God. When you pray, you are bringing your consciousness up to a God consciousness.

Speak this aloud to you,

> *"My Father and I are one.*
>
> *All that my Father is, I am.*
>
> *All that the Father has is mine."*

Say it again and this time, savor it. Taste the word like a fine meal. You must say these words into yourself until you believe it in every fiber of your being. Repeat after me,

> *"The complete nature of God moves within me."*

Again, what is the nature of God? Absolute Good. So, absolute good moves within you right now and always if you just remember it. God moves through you, to do for you all that you need and desire. Meditate on it, concentrate on it, digest the reality of it, accept it thoroughly, and think on it deeply. Put the "Great Me" in control, and keep your mind stayed on your Father, your instant and constant supply.

Make it firm in your mind. Work at really knowing it. Hold onto an attitude of accepting and appropriating (take possession and make use of exclusively), the supply you have just uncovered and set in motion. How? By your prayer and meditation you put the Universe on notice as to your power and your preparedness to accept only the very best.

Then, with the directions of the Christ in you, your good will know and obey. You cannot be resisted when your Christ Light shines.

Refuse to act, think, speak, react to or most importantly listen to or with anyone in anyway to anything except the truth. I am not saying you should go around calling everyone a liar and causing confusion. Use "not" a lot. I got this from the children. When it's not true, when it's not God like, tell your "not" your prosperity work is about you; not what anybody else thinks or says unless you accept it. Your subconscious mind doesn't know a thing about, *"you were just kidding or joking."* It always believes and does what you tell it without question, opinion, reservation or decision.

Every created thing is first an idea in mind and comes into existence through the spoken word. The word is the expression of an idea. Every word of lack and limitation is an indication of a false belief, a wrong answer. For prosperity you need a true idea, a right answer. When you speak words of lack, hard luck or limitation of any kind, you give them your power to use it against you. It is a form of suicide. Your words are the culminating power of your thoughts. Your words give form to your ideas. They pass the idea on to other minds causing them to form mental images. Your thoughts are the creative actions of your mind.

"Man decrees; God fulfills." You need to speak the right words, to decree. A decree is an authoritative order having the force of law. God's part is to establish in our lives, worlds, and affairs fulfillment of our works. Every day, instead of complaining, decree words of courage, hope, confident expectation, patience, peace, love, joy, appreciation, health, wealth, wondrousness, and excitement of ownership of your desires. Why? Because your thoughts and words must correlate properly for the right results.

Next step: get ready for your good. Prepare for your success. You do that by meeting the situation at hand now, with whatever you have to work with, in a joyous, confident way. You already have what you need to begin where you are right now whether you believe it or not. Wherever you are now is the perfect place to start, for this is the fullness of time. *"Be ye not deceived, God is not mocked."* I don't know what is in your heart but the Father does. And if it is not real inside of you, what I am saying will not work for you. But if you are really ready, if it is real inside of you, you cannot fail. Prepare to receive. Preparing shows active faith. Preparation stimulates your interest. Preparation shows that you have gotten rid of doubt and fear. Expectation is preparation. *"He that sows sparingly reaps sparingly."* The first step to receiving, is giving.

"Every man shall give as he is able, according to the blessing the lord thy God, which He has given thee. Give

to him that asks thee, and from him that would borrow of you, turn not away."

Deuteronomy 16:17

Jesus talking in Matthew 5:42, *"Give to him that asks you and from him that would borrow of you, turn not away."*

Luke 6:38, *"Give and it shall be given unto you; good measure, pressed down, and shaken together, and running over, shall men give into your bosom. For with the same measure that you mete withal, it shall be measured to you again."*

The best gift you have is you. Give to God and your fellowman of your true self; of the Christ inside of you. You are a spiritual being, living in a spiritual world, governed by spiritual laws. Your Father has put you here to express through, as you put into practice, your power to be fruitful and multiply.

The results are guaranteed if you are willing to be obedient to His words of instructions. Satisfaction guaranteed.

THE FOURTH PROSPERITY
COMMANDMENT

The Fourth commandment is *"Remember the Sabbath Day and keep it Holy. Six days shalt thou labor, and do all thy work; but the seventh day is the Sabbath of the Lord, in it thou not do any work, thou, nor thy son, nor thy daughter, thy manservant, nor maidservant. Nor thy castle, nor thy stranger that is within thy gates; wherefore the Lord has blessed, the Sabbath Day, and hallowed it."*

Exodus 20:8-11

Metaphysically speaking, the Sabbath is the consciousness that we have fulfilled the Divine Idea, both in thought and act. The Sabbath of the Lord has nothing to do with any day of the week. God did not make days or weeks, nor has He darkened His clear concepts of truth by the time element. Time is a human invention. The Sabbath is a very certain definite thing.

The true Sabbath is that state of spiritual attainment where we cease from all personal effort and all beliefs in our own works, and rest in the consciousness that as John 14:10 tells us, *"The Father abiding in Me is doing the work."* The Sabbath is the state of mind we enter into or we acquire when we go into the silence of our own soul, into the realm of spirit. The Sabbath is where we find true rest and peace. The seventh day means the seventh or perfect stage of your spiritual enfoldment. Seven is a mystical number used often in the Bible (494 times to be exact). Seven indicated perfection, that which is finished perfectly. The steps we have taken so far have brought us to this point. When we lay hold of the indwelling Christ, the Savior, we are raised from the Adam consciousness into the Christ consciousness, which is the seventh stage of our enfoldment: Perfection. The Fourth Prosperity Commandment, Thou shall let go and let God do it. Get out of the way and sit down on your faith and prepare to receive. Sabbath is a time of rest.

In every demonstration there is a time for rest; times for cessations from outer activity while you go to complete reliance on God and His laws. Remember we are all dealing with stages of enfoldment. The seven steps of creation outline a process. Metaphysically speaking (and we are metaphysicians here), we see beyond the physical into the spiritual, is that correct?

When you have sincerely put your mind, heart, and hands into a project, then you must let go and let God breathe life into it so it can become a living form. Keeping the Sabbath holy is creating new patterns of living. No more panic, doubt, or inhibitions but the new understanding that the spiritual "pause that refreshes" is equally as important as the work you are achieving. Keeping the Sabbath means disciplining yourself to regular periods of thankful prayer and meditation. To do all that you do, in the awareness of inner power, with frequent silences, to remember your oneness with the divine flow; you need creative resting. You need plugging in to the divine action that makes the physical possible and vital.

Say this out loud,

> *"I can rest now, God is in charge,*
> *and all is well and well indeed!"*

What does this do for you? The benefits of this procedure are:

† It increases your ability to make correct decisions.

† New creative ideas form.

† You will rise above the challenges of human relations.

† You will be in a good state of mind, free from all outside challenges, no matter who or what they are from.

† This is a beauty treatment no spa can match.

† It naturally improves you disposition.

† You will know that the presence of God is present wherever you are.

† The Universe will then find you more attractive and you will begin to be a part of "The Law of Attraction."

We refer to Jesus as our Wayshower. What was the way He showed us? He would go apart to pray and after a period of infilling, He would move through a period of intense activity of teaching, healing; then He would go away from everybody and everything to rest awhile. His resting period would in turn be followed by another cycle of work. In these periods of restfulness activity, we have many instances of His acknowledging His heavenly Father in Prayer before performing some miracle of healing that we would call a demonstration. Here is a law to rest in and on as you take your Sabbath.

The word "attract" means to draw. The Law of Attraction works at the unconscious levels, drawing prosperity to me. Affirm this aloud,

I am a magnetic field of mental influence.

I know that I attract to me what I am subconsciously thinking and feeling more than what consciously I say I want.

I attract according to my dominant thoughts and feelings. I truly believe my Father and I are one, so I can let go and let God do it.

I am enjoying that, and feeling it deeply in gratitude. Taking this Sabbath proves that I am not worried, that I have faith in God handling what has to be handled.

THE FOURTH PROSPERITY COMMANDMENT

By disciplining myself to regular periods of prayer and meditation I know I attract to me things to which I give a great deal of thought.

So I think about the desires of my heart and need of my mind, my body and my being.
I thank God for He is so good to me, blessing me constantly."

Here is information on the Sabbath:

Christian theologians who thought it more fitting to honor the "first day of the week" probably redesigned Sunday as the Sabbath Day.

When Jesus was resurrected from the dead, the Scots and the Puritans developed Sunday. Jews kept the Sabbath on Saturday, beginning sundown on Friday. Among Christians, the Seventh-Day Adventists observe the Sabbath on Saturday. Saturday is the seventh day of the week. People have been conditioned to the church going habit, chiefly out of fear of not going. It has become a badge of conventional respectability. It is politically correct to be seen going to services on the Sabbath.

Q: *Why is service at 11:00 a.m.?*

A: To accommodate the farmers. 11:00a.m. is half way between milking times!

Dealing with the literal Sabbath Day, it was intended to help the Israelites to put stress on resting, for health, and on times for prayer and meditation for recreation. Jesus clarified its purpose in Mark 2:27-28, *"The Sabbath was made for man, and not man for the Sabbath. Therefore the son of man is Lord, also of the Sabbath."*

He is telling us the idea of the Sabbath on the level of consciousness, and not just as a set time of day or week! There is no time or space in God. Creation being a God-product, it does not deal with time. Creation deals with stages of enfoldment. The seven steps of creation outline a process.

THE FIFTH PROSPERITY COMMANDMENT

The Fifth Commandment: *"Honor your Father and mother, so that your days may be long in the land that the Lord your God is giving you.*

Exodus 20:12

"Thou shall deal honorably with God and all human instruments through whom God's good is manifest for you."

I am a miracle in the making through the Fifth Prosperity Commandment.

Have you heard God referred to as "Father, Mother God"? Your biological mother was your transportation from the outer spiritual world to this world. Your biological father was the factor that God chose to start the formation of the transported object or item. God is your real father and mother.

Malachi 3: 8-12, *"Will a man rob God? Yet you have robbed Me, but you say wherein have we robbed Thee? In tithes and offerings. Ye are cursed with a curse for you have robbed Me, even this whole nation. Bring ye all the tithes into the storehouse, that there may be meat in Mine house, and prove Me now herewith, saith the Lord of Hosts, if I will not open you the windows of heaven, and pour out on you a blessing that there shall not be room enough to receive it. And I will rebuke this devourer for your sakes, and he shall not destroy the fruits of your ground. Neither shall your vines cast her fruit before the time in the field, saith the Lord of Hosts. And all nations shall call you blessed. For ye shall be a delightsome land, saith the Lord of Hosts."*

This is so clear to me it needs no explanation, but just in case you don't really, really understand it, we will reason it out together. Let's get some definitions clear so we understand exactly what we are talking about. First: Ground, is metaphysically a substance (substance is God), in His spiritual wholeness. Nation, metaphysically is an aggregation of thoughts in your mind, that are to be instructed through your God-given faculties. Your faculties are also your powers:

† **Faith** = Peter = Center of Brain
† **Love** = John = Back of your Heart
† **Strength** = Andrew = Lower Back
† **Wisdom** = James = Pit of the Stomach
† **Power** = Philip = Root of the Tongue
† **Imagination** = Bartholomew = Between the eyes
† **Understanding** = Thomas = Front of the Brain
† **Will** = Matthew = Center of the Brain
† **Order**=James= Navel
† **Zeal** = Simon = The Back of the Head
† **Purity / Elimination** = Thaddaeus = Abdomen
† **Life Conserver** = Judas = Generative Function

The subconscious realm in us has twelve great centers of action, with twelve presiding egos or identities. When we are developing out of mere personal consciousness, into spiritual consciousness, we begin to *train* deeper and larger powers. Each of these twelve department heads has control of a certain function. Upon the rock of faith you build your church. Church is derived from a Greek word meaning the Lord's house. Your individual consciousness is your "Lord's House." The church of Christ is your spiritual consciousness.

Upon the Rock of Faith you build yourself. And you fill your church with love. God is Love. From that church, and in that church you find and use your strength, wisdom, power, imagination, understanding, will, order, zeal, elimination and life conserver in any combination necessary. You got that?

Land, metaphysically is your consciousness unfolding at different levels from the invisible to the visible. Every reference to land has to do with various stages of awareness within you: plains, wilderness, deserts, plateaus, the Far Country, mountains, caves, islands, firmament, hills and valley. With this understanding, disobedience to the ordinances of God puts us in the position for curses. Curse: That which brings the causes of evil, injury or calamity. To eliminate the curse the Father is saying to us that we must change in order to rebuke the curse.

We must change to another stage of awareness and get in with the program. The program will not change and get in line with us. Thank God!

Storehouse: A place or building in which goods are stored; a warehouse; an abundant source or supply.

"Bring your tithes into the storehouse. Bring your tithes into the warehouse, into the source of supply (God is the source of abundant supply), *so that there will be meat in My house."* God is a spirit and He does not eat. So, what is meat to God? God's meat is your obedience, your love, your honest dealing with Him, *"your faith and prove Me herewith."*

Check me out right now. *"Saith the Lord of hosts, see for yourself if I will not open the windows of heaven* (inside of you where the Christ lives). *And pour out on you a blessing; there shall not be room enough to receive it. And I will rebuke the devourer for your sake."*

Devour: to destroy; to consume; to take in greedily with the senses or mind; to engulf.

Rebuke: reprimand, check, turn away, control.

"And He shall not destroy the fruits of your ground;" the fruits of awareness within you, your ideas, your dreams and plans. Trouble, confusion and anxiety can make you

lose sight of your conscious awareness. God won't let the devourer do that to you with appearances.

"Neither shall your vines cast her fruit before the time in the field, saith the Lord."

The ideas you are consciously aware of will not be entered into too soon, before they are ripe and ready to be executed. You won't keel going off, half-cocked, not fully prepared because you are listening to and have faith in the promises of God. Your faith gives you the patience; you wait on God to make your move. *"All nations shall call you blessed: because you will be a delightsome land, saith the Lord of Hosts."* You got that? Enter The Law of Compensation.

Be not deceived, God is not mocked: for whatsoever a man soweth, that he shall also reap. He that soweth to his flesh, shall, of the flesh reap corruption: but he that soweth to reap the spirit shall of the spirit reap everlasting. Galatians 6:7-8

The Law of Compensation is to return full value for what we receive always. The Law of Compensation is a law of balance. It means a balance of that quality or service that is extended to another. This law produces its own exactness as a rule of action. Balance, which is order, is God's first law. We are free agents to choose the method of procedure in our lives. The Law helps those who help themselves. The Law of Compensation always acts that way. You can depend on it.

The Law will not change. It doesn't need to. Success or prosperity does not need to be made, it already is. The change or changes must be made in you.

EXAMPLE: If you are adding 2 + 2 and getting 9, you are miscalculating. There is nothing wrong with the principles of mathematics. If your life is not as prosperous and happy and healthy as you deserve, desire it to be, as you are designed by God to be; you are miscalculating. Prosperity, happiness and healthiness are your inherited rights. You express them in your life when you use The Law correctly. The Law of Compensation will perform as it is designed to, no matter what you do. So, if you do not immediately return full value, your subconscious mind moves toward establishing balance, and if not now, sometime, somewhere, in someway; which is not always at a time when we desire to balance. Or when we can balance without great hassles that what is due to be paid presents itself. So the curse is activated.

Proverbs 3:9-10, *"Honor the Lord with your substance and with your first fruits of all your increase: So shall your barns be filled with plenty, and your presses shall burst out with new wine."*

Tithing is obeying this injunction, this commandment, this directive, this order.

The Hebrews of the Old Testament gave double and triple tithes, as did the ancient Egyptians. The Hindu's gave a tenth of their possessions as a tithe, while requiring their poor to pay 20%. The Hindu's thought that the poor needed a double portion of tithing power in order to rise above their conditions.

Tithing is a power that is already inside you. Tithing releases that power into a particular direction. Successful living and the good that is your divine right requires more than just the mechanics of giving a tithe to God's work. It is the spiritual power that you apply to tithing that makes it truly successful.

You must release your tithe with ease, without fear or concern, no strings and no negative thoughts, with an attitude of gratitude. To honor the Lord with your substance is to do inner service, to acknowledge His presence in prayer, praise, and worship. Tithing is honoring God with your finest fruits.

In the "Prosperity Commandments," by Georgiana Tree West, there is this, which is worth thinking about, *"We gladly accept from God, but we are prone to forget that there is something justly due to Him from us. When making a demonstration, we are accepting God's Laws working and on behalf, when the demonstration is completed, we must pay what is justly due God if we would deal honorably with God."*

THE FIFTH PROSPERITY COMMANDMENT

Will a man rob God? Yet you have robbed me! But you say wherein have we robbed thee? In tithes and offerings.
Malachi 3:8

Tithing is a form of worship. There is no better, surer way to Thank God for your blessing, and to acknowledge God as your source of supply than tithing. Tithing is accounting to God for what you have received.

Ten is the number of increase. So we give ten percent to increase our receiving of our blessings. Don't misunderstand this. You cannot bargain with God. You own nothing. What you do is obey. And therefore since you are doing what God has told you to, you then exercise your rights to the benefits He has in store for you.

"Give and it shall be given to you. Pressed down, shaken together, and running over shall men give into your bosom. For the same measure that your mete withal it shall be measured to you again." Luke 6:38

Jesus is talking here about person to person. Let me say this, the problem with most of your giving is that:

† It is not freely done.
† You expect your return from the person you gave it to.

It does say to give and it shall be given unto you. It doesn't say give and it shall be given to you by the person you gave to. Why limit your gifts to such a singular market? God is extravagant because He has so much to give, and He is your source of return for your gifts.

In order to become a millionaire and to hold onto your health and in harmony, in peace, and fulfillment; you have to begin to respect God enough to obey what He says and to do it willingly and freely. Trust Him enough to know He will not leave you, nor forsake you. He will supply your every need because He is your sufficiency in all things.

"Not what we are sufficient of ourselves to think that anything as of ourselves; but our sufficiency is of God, who also has made us able ministers of the New Testament. Not of the letter, but of the spirit, for the letter killith, but the spirit givith life."   2 Corinthians 3:5-6

"But my God shall supply all your needs according to His riches in glory by Christ Jesus."   Philippians 4:19

"And God is able to make all grace abound toward you: that you, always having all sufficiency in all things, may abound to every good works."   2 Corinthians 9:8

So, what is this all coming down to Rev. Della?

† If we want to reap, we must sow.
† Whatever we sow will produce after its own kind.
† Don't let nobody fool you baby, that's the way it goes, because that's the way God planned it.
† If you don't tithe, you are robbing God.

THE FIFTH PROSPERITY COMMANDMENT

† If you rob God, you break The Law.

† If you try to break The Law, it will break you because The Law cannot be broken; it is the Word of God.

† In order to reap, you must sow in fertile ground.

† You must sow with ease and with gratitude.

† We must sow in the spirit, not just the letter. For the letter kills, and the spirit is the giver of life.

† Whatever you are getting from life is yours. It belongs to you.

These are the seeds you have sown and you are reaping the fruits of your sowing. You cannot have it both ways. It is your way or God's way; it has to be this or that. Alter your mind right now. Dig up the old nonproductive ground and sow seeds of plenty with the energy of your mind and your mouth. Love, happiness, joy, health; and that's the crop you will grow, for it is by the design of the one power and one presence, God.

Seeds reproduce after their own kind. The Law of Compensation is your law and mine. God gave it to us to govern our good. Be fair with God and use The Law of Compensation to make your life a better place to live in.

THE SIXTH PROSPERITY COMMANDMENT

I am a miracle in the making through
"The Sixth Prosperity Commandment."

You shall not kill.

"Thou shall not kill" is the Sixth Commandment. You shall not take your wealth out of circulation. You have heard the expression, *"There is more than one way to skin a cat"*? There is more than one way to kill. You can kill a reputation with slander and lies. You can kill someone's dream. You can kill your dreams. You can kill confidence; yours and that of your spouse or children. Evil words and thoughts are killers. Stagnation is a death filled thing. Lack of circulation is the cause of stagnation. Some of you are locked in a warped time zone.

Warp: to turn or twist out of shape, to turn aside from a true, correct or natural course.

You have thought what you think and have acted the way that you act so long it has become your natural course. Your normal mean, and that course is incorrect. Your understanding and therefore methods are twisted out of shape, they are not what God has designed your life to be. When you hoard, you hold on to your money, you go against the natural grain of money. Money is reproduced by the circulating of it. When you circulate the gifts God has given you, those gifts increase your life; in proportion to the increase of value in the lives of others.

"For with the same measure that we mete withal it shall be measured to you again."   Luke 6:38

If you need love, give some love.   If you need understanding, understand somebody. If you need peace, bring peace as a gift wherever you go.   If you need money, give money to somebody. If you need kindness, be kind to somebody. If you want success and prosperity, you must use to the utmost what is already yours. Stagnation is death. Circulation is life. So if you don't want to kill your prosperity, do not take your wealth out of circulation. Now let's clear up this passage of the Bible so that it can no longer confuse and contain you.

"For the love of money is the root of all evil; which while some coveted after, they have erred from the faith and pierced themselves through with so man sorrows.   But thou, o man of God, flee these things; and follow after righteousness, godliness, faith, love, patience and meekness.   1 Timothy 6:10-11

The love of money will make you pierce yourself through with many things that bring you sorrow."

The use of money is the operating of the barter system. Bartering has been in practice since the beginning of time.

It was bread, beads, chickens, eggs, cows and sheep. It was silver. It was gold. It *was* salt.

Centuries ago when salt was scarce and modern methods of processing were unknown, salt became a medium of exchange. Our term "salary" derives from the Latin word "Sal" which means salt. In those days they paid their soldiers and workers in salt.

"Ye are the salt of the earth; but if the salt have lost its savour where with shall it he salted. It is therefforth good for nothing but to be cast out, and trodden underfoot of men." Matthew 5:13

Salt was precious and some people kept it badly. "It" being mined salt, which is dry instead of wet sea salt, kept incorrectly; it dried up and had no seasoning power.

When money is put out and used in its proper manner and place, it becomes an outer symbol of God's abundance. We are operating our recognition of its purpose as exchange of value for value received. Money is a symbol of God's plentiful, luxuberant, profuse, lavish beauty and abundance. Money is God in action. We define prosperity as being able to do what I want to do at the instant I want to do it; to the extent that I wish to do it, as long as I desire to do it, despite what my bank account reveals, or any other document, set of circumstances or situations reveal. Money is a vital part of the necessary circulatory system of this age. You must understand it is a spiritual idea. It is necessary for the economic health of us all.

We must remember always, money is a circulatory system created to be circulated.

What I am saying is, when we hoard it, it is because we believe there is not enough flow and there is not going to be enough. What you believe is what you receive. If you say there is not enough, you are absolutely correct; for you there cannot be enough because you do not believe there is enough. Enter prayer and praise! Prayer is a common union with God, a communion! Praise is an expression of warm approval or admiration; it is the extolling of a deity, to exalt, to worship.

David knew about praise: Psalm 34:1, *"I will bless the Lord at all times; His praise shall continually be in my mouth."*

Jesus tells us and this is true, money or no money: *"if thou canst believe, all things are possible to him that believes,"* Mark 9:23

*"If any man thirst, let him come unto Me and drink, he that believes on Me, as the scripture has said out of his belly (*his wisdom*) shall flow rivers of living water."*

John 7:37-38

The rivers of the living waters are the rivers of life. When we are in and on faith, when we really believe and make an intimate connection between our mind and the Father's mind, we enter into the river of life.

"But with out faith it is impossible to please God; for he that comes to God must believe that He is a rewarder of them that diligently seek Him."   Hebrew 11:6

"If you abide in Me, and My words abide in you, you shall ask what you will, and it shall be done unto you."
                                                                    John 15:7

"Therefore I say unto you, what things so ever you desire, when you pray, believe that you receive them, and you shall have them."   Mark 11:24

"Whatsoever we ask, we receive of Him, because we keep His commandments, and do those things that are pleasing in His sight."   1 John 3:22

The purpose of praise is to awaken in ourselves a higher realization of the omnipresence and power of God. Prayer and praise change us not God...the mental attitude that praise sets up, stimulates, quickens, and whirls into action. Finally, establishing in character, the ideals of which they are the vehicle. Through an inherent Law of Mind action, we increase whatever we praise. Everything responds to praise...animals, men, women, children, flowers. You can praise want and seeming insufficiency into supply and support. It will be circulated in my bank account, also my pocket book. More than in any other place, it must be in my attitude about money.

I must believe:

† I am in a Universe, which is self-sustaining.
† I am a part of this self sustaining Universe.
† The creative process that causes the Universe to be self-sustaining must likewise be in my affairs and cause my affairs to be self sustaining.
† I will be wise in the use of my money, not be abusive with money.
† I will be receptive to the idea of money.
† If I will not be obsessed with money and not forget my source and my supply, I shall have money.

I must know all things work together for the good of these who love the Lord, and nothing good is withheld from those who love God. Nothing good is withheld from me. Money is an outer symbol of God's defense for me against lack and limitation. The person who has money and uses it intelligently, keeping it in circulation unselfishly, and is getting enjoyment out of it, is rich. The one who has it and hoards it, or the person who uses it only for selfish purposes, is still poor no matter the dollar amount that person has. The person who has faith in God as the never failing resource and the constant supply, uses money fearlessly and joyfully, knowing that God *is,* his or her, abundant source and supply.

You have to come to the place where you no longer have to think about money. Why? You have arrived at a subconscious conviction that you will always have money. And so, you will always have money, because you are subjectively convinced.

This is financial freedom. Money does not come from work necessarily. There are business executives who actually work just two hours a day, a couple of days a week. They take six-week vacations whenever they desire, and yet they receive their enormous salaries on a yearly basis. They are considered worth that kind of money and treatment.

What are you worth? (Which may or may not be what you say you think you are worth, because *"as a man thinks in his heart so is he."* That is The Law.) We are what we think, not necessarily what we say we are. You have got to convince your mind. Jesus always asked those that needed help *"Do you believe I can do this?"* If the answer was yes, He said all right. It is conviction, which made the demonstration. You demonstrate your money substance through your subjective conviction. It must be a strong and fixed belief. It has to be so real in your mind that it cannot be affected by the external world. Jesus, *"Judge not by the appearances, judge by the righteous judgment."*

Wealth is a relative thing, and one reality about the Universal Mind (God), He always gives us plenty and to spare and to share. God works under The Law of Abundance with no secondary Law of Lack and Limitation.

Hear me good now. This is where you do as your Father does. You cannot work under The Law of Abundance with a subconscious pattern of limitation. It yields no results. You cannot, on the surface say that you desire plenty of money, you deserve to be a millionaire, but your subconscious pattern is a $60 pattern. The Universe takes us at our valuation, and each one of us needs to increase the consciousness of our own self-evaluation, and our evaluation of money. What I am talking about is confidence, not conceit. Confidence is positive; conceit is negative, due to lack of real appreciation on one's self. When you begin to have this confidence, money will start to appear in your experiences. The great law of "give and take."

Give, then you can take or claim abundance from the rich Universe. Why? Because through your act of giving you have opened the channel through which the universal supply can pour forth to you in appropriate form. Sharing your supply insures continuation of your supply in practical ways. You will find sharing and expectancy are the beginning of financial increase. By not giving, you stop your own receiving of greater supply because you are violating the universal Laws of Prosperity.

"One man gives freely yet grows all the richer; another withholds what he should give and only suffers want." "A liberal man will be enriched, and one who waters himself will be watered."   Proverbs 11:24-25

The Bible points out clearly that when you give you are always protected from the negative experiences of life; that when you are not giving that you submit yourself to the negative forces of hard times, bad crops, poor business, theft, accidents, ill health, all the "unwanteds." YOU can expect inharmony on all levels of your life because you are going against (violating), The Law of the Universe. You are not big enough or bad enough to go up against God and The Laws of His mighty Universe.

"Fear not little flock; it is your Father's good pleasure to give you the kingdom."   Luke 12:32

It is your Father's pleasure to give you the kingdom. The question is, are you willing to do what is necessary to receive the kingdom and all of its benefits? I have prepared a partnership agreement for you if you are really, I mean really, ready to work at receiving your prosperity. Sign this partnership agreement. Deal honestly with God and there is no possibility that your good will not be yours and that more abundantly.

Just signing it with your physical signature won't get it done. You have to sign it with your heart, mind, being, physicality, power of your convictions and your determination to do the best you can.

If for some reason you fall short, you will get up and start all over again. This is personal and private. Your "partnership agreement" should only be handled by you.

THE SEVENTH PROSPERITY COMMANDMENT

"You shall not commit adultery"

Adulterate: To make impure, spurious, or inferior by adding extraneous or improper ingredients, to pollute.

Spurious: Lacking authenticity or validity; counterfeit; false; similar in appearance but unlike in structure or function.

"You shall not abase your wealth to idle or evil uses." You will have to clean up your act to deal with God. He deals in purity or at least the constant attempts to be as pure as you can on the level of consciousness you are living on at this time. You cannot go above the present level of your consciousness until you raise the level of your consciousness. You will have to strive for purity. You cannot be led to adultery for any seeming gain, any comfort or benefit of any form; because it will be a false spurious situation or circumstance, carrying with it and leaving behind it confusion, pain, grief, and/or sorrow. You need to maintain purity of thoughts and actions. We must control the sense appetites. We must, knowing our supply source is God, be good stewards.

"Moreover it is required in steward, that a man be found faithful."   1 Corinthians 4:2

"Then the Lord said, 'Who then is that faithful and wise steward, whom his Lord shall make ruler over his household, to give them their portion of meat in due season, blessed is that servant, whom his Lord when he comes shall find so doing. Of truth I say unto you that He will make him ruler over all that he has. But and if that servant says in his heart my Lord delays His coming, and that servant begins to beat the men servants and maiden, and to eat and drink and be drunken; The Lord of that servant will come in a day when he lookith not for Him, and at an hour when he is not aware, and will cut him in sunder, and will appoint him his portion with the unbelievers."   Luke 12: 42-46

Being faithful to God is wise. If you are wise you will be faithful, then, in God's own time, which is your appointed time, God will make you ruler of your house.

House: the house that God builds and dwells in is you and me.

"For you are the temple of the living God, and God has said, 'I will dwell in them, and walk in them and I will be their God, and they shall be my people."

2 Corinthians 6:16,

O.k., how do I do the things you are speaking of Rev. Della? There are three laws that enter here, The Law of

Change, The Law of Adaptation and The Law of Mental Acceptance.

Most people think of change as the giving up of something. In the Bible, the passing away of one leader and the rising of another symbolized the changes through which a progressive person passes. You want this leader of lack and limitation, of trials and tribulations, of confusion and anxiety, to be replaced by your loving Father, whose will for you is peace of mind, love, joy, happiness and prosperity.

Change is a success power. Success is the natural order of the Universe, ordained by God as a force for good, to replace the effects of this world with divine reality. The human nature of man is to resist change, but the spiritual nature insists on change. If you have ever said *"There's got to be something better in life than this." "I wish something would happen. "Life is boring." "I am in a rut."* These feelings are telling you that you need a change.

The restlessness and dissatisfaction you are feeling is telling you that you are at the end of a cycle in your growth and progress. Not only are you restless and dissatisfied, what was wonderful is no longer adequate and you no longer are successful with it or at it. Your soul is reaching out toward greater possibilities.

That is why you are reading this prosperity series, so you will acknowledge, confess, and admit the existence, the reality of the truth. The truth is when you accept God's will in your life, you set The Law of Mental Acceptance into motion. In your human existence you may not be able to mentally accept this greater experience. You cannot have what you cannot accept. That is why some people are prosperous and others are in "need more-ville." Those who are successful:

† Have used the prosperity Law of Mental Acceptance.

. † Released the past and their old ways.

† Accepted the possibility and the probability that God has something better to offer and they are ready to receive it.

To mentally accept your good is to change the way you think about it. Change your mind and you change your life. You gain more than you give up. You give up things and people that are not working for the good in your life. While you gain the will of God, which is absolute good and is always successful, your plan is not working. His plan cannot fail.

"Jesus increased in wisdom and in statue and in favor with God and men."   Luke 2:52

If you are following Jesus, you too must increase in wisdom and statue and find favor in God, and men.

Change is hard because you have become used to the practices that you are now using and you don't know for sure how this new plan or new way will turn out. You believe in someday, or when things get better, when the economy gets better, if my health holds out, after the elections if things change, when I get a little more money, when I get a better job. These are shelters that keep you from having to do anything. The only thing you can be certain of, pertaining to life that will always remain the same, is that there will be changes. You must be able to adapt to and with the change in order to bring your life in to harmony. The Law of Adaptability enters here.

Adapt: to make suitable by changing, to change without difficulty.

Adaptability is a mental action:
† When a need arises, do not panic.
† Jesus never rushed into anything, don't you rush into anything either.
† Whatever comes up, work it out on the inside of you with your "spiritual principle consciousness" in your thought and feeling nature first.
† Prepare inwardly then speak words of abundance.
† Then start by using what you have no matter how little you think it is. Believe it or not you

already have on hand what you need to meet the demands that are made upon you. Treat the available supply as the desired supply.

† Take your rough circumstance, your bodily conditions, your human affairs just as they are, and hold them in your mind.

† Begin to praise them, bless them, give thanks to your all providing God, that within them is the peace and health and success that is your divine right.

† You may think there is not enough, maybe there is not enough of you, but there is more than enough God.

† Think a new thought, read a Bible verse, say a prayer, read an inspirational book, sing an old hymn or gospel song, meditate and declare the victory.

† Do not reject your good because it is not in the form you would like it to be, or the person you would like to bring to you does not bring it to you.

As you adapt in these ways to both the seen and unseen good at hand, the desires of your heart begin to materialize more and more as results. This is the prosperity Law of Adaptability.

Remember there is no hope that ever stirs within us that God doesn't have the actual fulfillment of that hope for us – but in His own way. Don't just hear me say that. Take it as the truth it is and apply it to your life. You too can change the waters of your life to the finest wines. You can walk the water, you can heal what is sick, you can raise the dead; for you have enough faith. And God pays on demand of our faith, even if our faith is only the size of a mustard seed. I am in partnership with my Father God. We have a covenant.

I must, of course, do my part because my Father never fails to do His part.

† I will keep my life pure.

† I will avoid, like the plague, all things and people who are not God like.

† I am faithful; I am worthy of trust.

† I am constantly reliable, God can count on me.

† Change is a success power. I am changing! I replace the appearance and effects of this world with divine reality.

† Following these Principles make me adaptable to enjoy the God-given benefits

† I accept God's will in my life and am setting The Law of Mental Acceptance in motion.

THE EIGHTH PROSPERITY COMMANDMENT

The Eighth commandment is *"Thou shall not steal."*

The Eighth Prosperity Commandment: *"You shall not seek something for nothing."*

To steal is to take without right or permission, generally in a surreptitious way.

Surreptitious: performed, made up, or acquired by secret clandestine or stealth means.

"Thou shall not covet thy neighbors house, thou shall not covet thy neighbors wife, nor his manservant, nor his maidservant, nor his ox, nor his ass, nor anything that is thy neighbors." Exodus 20:17

"For the wicked boasts of his hearts desire and, blessed the covetous, who thee Lord abhorres. The wicked, through the pride of his countenance, will not seek after God; God is not in all his thoughts." Psalm 10:3-4

We steal because we covet! Earlier we learned about The Law of Compensation.

Compensation: equal return for that which is given.

"As a man soweth, so shall he reap." There is no reaping for you from stealing because you haven't

sown any producing seeds. What you've sown, or given, is sorrow, misery and hurt. Therefore that is what you will reap, because that action too is covered by The Law. The Law, *"Things produce after their own kind."*

"And God made the beast of the Earth after their own kind, and the cattle after their kind, and everything that creeps upon the Earth after his own kind: and God said that is good."   Genesis 1-26

Thou shall not steal!

"Then He said unto me, 'This is the curse that goes forth over the face of the whole earth: For every one that steals shall be cut off.'"   Zechariah 5:3

"Let him that stole, steal no more; but rather let him labor, working with his hands the thing which is good, that he may have to give to him that he needs."

Ephesians 4:28

What are you talking about Rev. Della? I have never stolen anything in my life! Let's look at that statement.

Do you stretch your lunch hour or coffee break? How about falsifying sick days? If you have an expense account, do you pad it? At work, do you hold back on your productiveness? Do you take credit for things you haven't done? Are you into get, get, get, and never give, give, give? Do you enjoy the lunches and never pick up the check? Do you tithe? Do you add adultery to your theft by adulterating the truth of God's abundance by believing there isn't enough?

When you steal, you conform to lack and limitation. When you steal, you do that because you believe that there is not enough and you will not have any unless you take somebody else's. When you steal, you conform for yourself that God is unable to supply your needs. When you steal a thought, for example, you are saying to your mind, "Mind, you are not capable of thinking," so I will take this thought and name it mine.

If you make $10 an hour for 8 hours, you make $80 a day. In 5 days, you make $400.00 per week before taxes. When you stretch your lunch hour an extra 20 minutes, you steal $3.33 (16.66666666 or 16 and a ½ cents each minute). When your stretch is an hour, you steal $10. Let's say you stretch it 20 minutes 5 times a month. You steal $16.65. So for less than 20 dollars over a month's time, you give up your integrity and your honesty. You steal $80.00 every time you falsify a sick day. You steal on a regular basis when you pad your expense account.

When you enjoy lunches but never pick up the check, you lose friends and their opinion of you comes to the reality that with you it's "get, get, get", and no "give, give, give". They feel used and you lose.

Adultery and stealing make you unable to open your mind and feel worthy of your spiritual inheritance. When you steal you find you cannot trust anybody. Why? Because you steal! We judge people by ourselves, so you think everybody steals.

You become suspicious and sometimes paranoid, depending on how big a thief you are. You don't expect to prosper, and you are right not to expect to prosper for you are doing everything you can to keep from prospering. You need to raise your level of consciousness. You need to obey the eighth prosperity commandment. "Stop trying to get something for nothing." You don't have to.

There is plenty and your good will suit you perfectly, while mine will be horrible for you, on you, in you, and around you. You are living in a "widow's consciousness," which is a belief in lack. In Jesus' time a widow had no rights to buy, sell or own, to inherit, or transact her business affairs. The story of the widow's mite is a story of one of the world's mightiest financial transactions. It is significant that just before His crucifixion He thought about and taught about prosperity. Out of all the offerings given in this treasure tale, the widow's mite impressed Jesus.

"And Jesus sat over against the treasury, and He beheld how the people cast money into the treasury; and many that were rich cast in much. And there came a certain poor widow, and she threw in two mites, which a farthing ½ cent. Jesus called unto Him His disciples, and said to

them: 'Verily I say unto you that this poor woman has cast more in than all they did cast in is of their abundance; but she of her want did cast in all that she had, even all her living."   Mark 12:41-44

Two mites are almost one penny. Through her drastic act of giving away her last two mites she was trying to break out of the belief in lack; trying to develop a prosperity consciousness. She was trying to provide herself with the divine protection and power she knew she lacked. She knew supply could be made to increase through sharing.

Instead of stealing it is necessary when you believe in a state of lack you must go a second mile to get out of that state of lack. You will have to do more than the average person. In order to break your thriving habit thoughts, and in order to prosper beyond your feelings that stealing is the only way. You must be willing not only to pray, but also to share whatever you already have, to show that you are capable of handling more. You show that you know God's supply is unlimited. You show that you are receptive to God's supply. You steal because you feel separated from your good, which is God. You steal from a feeling of being without worldly possessions and power.

The powers to acquire your own worldly possessions are in the Christ inside of you. You are going to have to dare to do something drastic if you are going to prosper. The widow gave out of deficit, not out of surplus. If you are stealing in any way, you are faced with a deficit. She, just as you, must put God first financially.

She gave in faith. Giving in faith prospers you. Your act of faith moves on the rich substance of the Universe, causing it to fill your life to overflowing with its abundance.

"When you come into thy neighbors vineyard, then thou mayest eat grapes to they fill at thine own pleasure; But thou shall not put any in thy vessel." Deuteronomy 23:24

I don't need to take your stuff. I can claim as much as I am capable of accepting of God's bountiful supply. Emerson said, *"In labor as in life there can be no cheating."* The thief steals from himself. The swindler swindles himself. Wealth is a manifestation of your state of mind. You cannot steal state of mind. You must consciously create it. Why steal a little of mine, when you can have all of yours? Why try something for nothing, when you can have your very own everything in abundance through the power of your faith, for God pays on the demand of your faith from His riches in glory.

THE NINTH PROSPERITY COMMANDMENT

Exodus 20:16, *"You shall not bear false witness against your neighbor."*

Witness: one that furnishes evidence, to be present at a transaction in order to attest to what took place, to be present at or have personal knowledge of, to attest to the legality or authenticity of, by signing your name.

False: contrary to fact or truth; without ground, incorrect; untruthful; without meaning or sincerity; deceiving; not keeping faith; treacherous.

"Thou shall not bear false witness against thy neighbor."

Gossip: trifling, often groundless rumor; usually of a sensational or intimate nature; idle talk.

Gossiper: a person who habitually engages in such talk, trivial chatty talk or writings.

"He that keeps his mouth keeps his life; but he that opens wide his lips shall have destruction."   Proverbs 13:3

"Whosoever keeps his mouth and his tongue keeps his soul from troubles."   Proverbs 21:23

THE NINTH PROSPERITY COMMANDMENT

Jesus speaking, *"A good man out of the good treasure of the heart brings forth good things; and an evil man out of evil treasure bring forth evil things. But I say unto you, that every idle word that men shall speak, they shall give account thereof in the Day of Judgment. For by thy words thou shall be justified and by thy word thou shall be condemned."* Matthew 12:35-36

The Ninth Prosperity Commandment: *"You shall not bear false witness against the source of your wealth."*

Stop lying on God! Stop saying there is not enough. Stop lying on yourself. Stop saying there is nothing that can be done, you don't know what to do, and you can't win. Stop saying you are not good enough, white enough, black enough, skinny enough, intelligent enough... whatever enough.

You are "all the enough" you need to be. But you keep bearing false witness and calling God a liar when it's you that is lying.

"If I will that he tarry till I come, what is that to thee; follow thou Me." John 21:22

Mind your own business, your own life, your own experiences.

"For He makes the sun to rise on the evil and on the good and sends the rain on the just and on the unjust."

Matthew 5:45,

If God is allowing whoever to do whatever, what business is that of yours? You just keep on your way; following what you know is the way, of your Wayshower Jesus Christ. It does not interest me who is sleeping with who or whom. I see images in my mind and the image of the bodies of some of you having sex is unbearable, and in some cases frightening. In order for sex to be interesting to me, I must be totally involved in it. I don't care in the least what your sexual persuasion is. I don't care how you got your money. Why would I clutter my mind with such junk? Why would I discuss what I have not seen, and have no evidence of? I can make conversation without discussing your business. I can speak of things of truth that I have evidence of that are worth my witnessing to.

I am not usually tempted to think in ways that are adverse to God, but in those instances which I am tempted, I remember my place and get back in it P.D.Q. Look at me, you can see that I do not accept lack of any good thing because that is bearing false witness against God. How can I teach you if I am a raga-muffin? How can I tell you happy prosperous loving marriages are available when every time I see you I am telling you what a dog my husband is, which is truly bearing witness to the falsest of false?

We are all prophets and we speak into our lives all day, everyday. Some of your relationships suffer from your prophecies. You bear false witness. What he/she does, is not who he or she is. You take what has been done and store it, stockpile it and place it in your arsenal. You use it as a tool.

I teach a workshop named, "I Am Woman Designed By God." A lady said she had been married for over twenty years; she had never trusted her husband. The reason being, something she found out, in his private papers, shortly after the wedding that she thought was horrible. So she never fully gave herself to this horrible-doing person she was married to. For over twenty years she had witnessed falsely to herself about her closest neighbor, her husband. She said that he was very happy. And though she had no complaints about his treatment of her, in fact he was "a good man." And she had never seen whatever it was she saw again.

She just couldn't forget what she had seen all those years ago. Whatever she saw, he was still "the son of God." If she really loved him and wanted to be happy, she would have found a way to deal with it then. Instead of living twenty years of lies and deceit. She should have in all those years, seen the Christ in him.

But she had let what she saw make her continue to see him as whatever it was she found.

The false witnessing to herself for whatever reason cheated her and him over twenty years of complete joyous happiness.

† It kept her from being completely happy.

† It has made her a liar and cheat, deceiving him for over twenty years.

† He had happiness because happiness is an inside job but he never had the fullness of the woman he loved.

We must learn to deal with each other for who and whose we really are. We are the sons of God in whom He is well pleased. And we can do very stupid things! We have to accept the truth about our neighbors and ourselves. We are going to making mistakes, but what we do is not who we are. We must bear truthful witness to who we are and understand that we are all one. We must understand that when I run you down, or hold a grudge against you, or lie to you, or deceive you in any way, I am doing it to myself because The Law never changes.

"For with the same measure you mete withal it shall be measured again unto you."　　　　　　　　Luke 6:38

THE NINTH PROSPERITY COMMANDMENT

I will not deny God's omnipresence, His omnipotence, and omni-science. I will not deny that wherever I am God is!

God and all His knowledge and power are where ever I am. It is available for my use backed by God's authority to use them for my highest good. I know this is true for me and I bear witness that this is also true for you.

Say this aloud:

The spirit of the Lord is upon us (me)

It is in us, (me)

Through us (me)

Giving to us (me)

I relinquish my will and understanding to the will and understanding of God's spirit for:

Instructions

Directions

Guidance

Definite action

My searching and finding the equipment, techniques, and corrections needed to do what the Father wants me to do.

I bear witness that this is the truth of my being and I accept completely for my neighbors, and myself that I am truly full of power by the spirit of the Lord and of righteous judgment and might.

I will not deny God's love and goodwill for me; nor His pleasure in giving me the Kingdom. So I will not falsely say I don't know what I am going to do. I am going to do what I am supposed to do, use the omni-science of God, the all-knowing knowledge of God.

I am going to the Christ inside of me and listen to the instruction, and then I am going to speak the truth into the situation or circumstance and with my power, domination, and mastery. I will subdue.

Bearing false witness example: You use your faculty of imagination as important as it is, with no evidence or personal knowledge. You imagine what I am doing, why I am doing it and with whom I am doing it with. You take an incident, a relatively minor occurrence, something you heard, something it seems like, something you feel about me from before, something it looks like; and you create (another of your gifts from God), a scenario. And then you use your zeal, and your strength to keep the lie alive. You even go so far sometimes to say you do it out of love.

You are having problems on your job. There is a benefit of some kind available. You hear a story about your opponent that could discredit him or her. It's low, but it might be the balancing point in your favor. You call forth your God-given faculties. You use the power of your tongue to insinuate and exaggerate with no proof, no personal knowledge; you haven't seen it so you are conveying false impressions, with your idle words.

You put your faith in deception. You go against wisdom., and you bear false witness. The Ninth Commandment is thou shall not bear false witness against your neighbor, and the Ninth Prosperity Commandment is you shall not bear witness against the source of your supply. Stop lying on God. Stop saying and acting like there is not enough; that He will not see to your needs if you ask Him and let Him. Stop lying on your neighbor. What he or she does is between them and God. Stop using gossip to be included in the conversation. Mind your own business. Learn some new topics. Stop lying to yourself that you can be successful bearing false witness.

Matthew 12:36, *"But I say unto you every idle word that men shall speak, they shall give account thereof in the Day of Judgment. For by their words thou shall be justified and by thy words you shall be condemned,"* so said Jesus. Watch your mouth!

THE TENTH PROSPERITY COMMANDMENT

The Tenth Commandment is, *"Thou shall not covet thy neighbor's house, thou shall not covet thy neighbor's wife, nor his manservant, nor his maidservant, nor his ox, nor his ass, nor anything that is thy neighbors."*

The Tenth Prosperity Commandment is,
"Thou shall not limit thyself by coveting that which is another's."

"Thou shall claim thy own." With this commandment, we pass from the realm of effects to the realm of causes. The first four Commandments have to do with right action toward God. The last six Commandments have to do with the right action towards men.

Covetousness is the mental cause from which the outer effects of lying, stealing, adultery, killing, unkind and unjust treatments are fed. The root cause of covetousness is our failure to look to God as our source of supply.

You see something. You want it, but in that wanting you fail to realize the ever-present God and His power is willing and will supply it to you through your faith if you ask Him and believe He will… So you don't need mine.

You make the mistake of thinking that what you see in the realm of form is the only possible fulfillment of your desire. You forget the power of God's supply is endless and that same form, or an even better one made to your own personal design, can be produced and reproduced forever and ever at infinitum by the demand of your faith.

When you covet, it is because you do not believe that there is enough to go around. As Jesus said, *"Let those with ears hear."* God's substance, God's supply is limitless. It only requires you to know, and know for sure, that you can have your own. You don't have to settle for somebody else's. When you really know that, through your trust in God you will see somebody else's not as a thing to covet, but as proof positive that it can be done. Anything God has already done can be done for you if you desire it having the faith to require it.

I used to sing a song, when I was younger that said, *"It's no secret what God can do. What He has done for others, He can do for you. With arms wide open He'll welcome you. It's no secret what God can do."* God has all this good stuff for you with your name on it. Whose fault is it if you don't take yours, which is designed for you, because you are looking over here coveting mine, which will neither fit nor suit you? And if you get it you won't be able to keep it in peace, because it doesn't belong to you.

When you covet you, misinterpret your desire. You cannot desire something that cannot exist for you. I did not say want. I said desire. Wants, wishes, and desires are all different. Desire is an insistent yearning, and anything that the heart yearns for, that is for your highest good, insistently is possible to obtain.

"As a man thinkith in his heart (his subconscious mind) *so is he* (or she)." You are not what you think you are. You are what you think. We are the out picturing of the sum total of our inner yearnings and desires. Our contract says clearly, *"What is done in the dark, will come out in the light."* So whatever is going on inside of you is what will be expressed on the outside in your life, world, and affairs.

When you suffer under the illusion that someone else has your stuff, or can take your stuff, you are ignorant of God's Law. Only God has what you want and He delivers on the demand of your faith. You do not want what I have anyway. It wouldn't make you feel good, because it is designed especially for me, my desires and my needs. If you had it, you would be surprised how much trouble it would be to you.

Because since it is not yours, you will not know what to feed it to make it grow. Desire is always the first indication of some good that God has for you. Desire is God tapping at the door of your heart saying I want to express this wondrousness through you! Why would you wrap your wondrousness in a ball of covetousness and bury it in the tomb of ignorance where there is no way for it to materialize? Sometimes you become so intent on striving to take something you want from someone else, that the entire situation gets out of hand and someone else, a third party steps in and takes the prize. God will not be stopped in the fulfillment of the things He wants to be brought forth. Because you are hanky pankying around out of the socket, seeking someone else's stuff, He gives the desire to another and produces through them.

Listen carefully and program this into your computer (your mind). This is for input. Mark it and save it. God is living intelligence and spiritual substance:

† Always willing

† Always ready

† More than able to respond to our call of faith

† God is a mind force that only needs the action of your mind as an instrument for His functioning

† Your faith furnishes the absolutely perfect condition under which God's spiritual substance moves, with resistless power to make manifest the thing we desire

† Your attitude has got to be, "My Christ self, the real constructive powerful self is desirous of, and working toward my highest good."

Why can I tell you this and ask you to believe this? Because our contract (The Bible), tells us this is the way to do it. *"All things work together for the good of those who love the Lord."* If I love the Lord with all my heart and soul, mind and body, strength and being; and I think and act that way. I am one of the ones that all things work together for the good of. Seems so simple to me. I cannot see how it could possibly be confusing. If I do not love the Lord, (loving is not something you say, loving is something you do, love is an action word!), if I do not love the Lord, I have a huge problem! It is simple to me.

You know the story of Joseph? How his brothers abused him, tried to kill him, and then had to return him to beg for food to keep them from starving? When they recognized Joseph as their brother, the one they had really, really treated badly, they tried to apologize to Joseph and he told them, *"You meant it for evil yet God meant it for good."* They coveted the affection their father had for Joseph.

Let me leave you with this:

Joseph metaphysically represents imagination. I can see how although his brothers persecuted him, he could continue, because his imagination was powerful and productive, he was able to remain a dreamer and was able to hold on to his high spiritual ideas. With those high spiritual ideas, he was able to see a brighter day coming although he did not know how or when. He survived his brothers, and the sense of darkness the forced upon him with their brutal actions.

Joseph was able to rise from distress and mistreatment by holding on to his dreams and his imagination and his faith in God. He rose from the depths to the heights. He became second only to Pharaoh and in God's time, he saw those who set out to kill him, have need to come to him in order to survive.

He did not seek revenge, he did not withhold from them, nor did he try to extract any other kind of payment or repentance. He accepted that whatever had happened, though it appeared evil, God in His magnificence had meant it for good and saw to it that it was for the good of all concerned.

Sometimes in our lives everything seems so wrong and so hard to bear that we lose our faith, our imagination, our high spiritual ideas and fall into a sense of darkness. But let me give you this: "All things work together for the good of those who love the Lord." The question then is do you love the Lord? If you love the Lord no matter how dark it seems, you can know for sure that God is going to protect you, elevate you. Know as Joseph knew, your brothers and sisters, so called friends, whosoever, may mean it for evil, but God means it for good.

When it seems as black as night, if you will just hold on until tomorrow everything is going to be all right.

GOD LOVE YOU AND HE WILL NEVER LEAVE YOU NOR FORSAKE YOU. IT IS HIS GOOD PLEASURE TO GIVE YOU THE KEYS TO THE KINGDOM.

THE 10 COMMANDMENTS OF
THE OLD TESTAMENT

† You shall have no other gods before Me.

† You shall not make for yourself a carved image--any likeness of anything that is in heaven above, or that is in the earth beneath, or that is in the water under the earth

† You shall not take the name of the LORD your God in vain.

† Remember the Sabbath day, to keep it holy.

† Honor your father and your mother.

† You shall not murder.

† You shall not commit adultery.

† You shall not steal.

† You shall not bear false witness against your neighbor.

† You shall not covet your neighbor's house; you shall not covet your neighbor's wife, nor his male servant, nor his female servant, nor his ox, nor his donkey, nor anything that is your neighbor's.

THE PROSPERITY COMMANDMENTS

† You shall look only to God for your good.

† You shall make no mental images of lack or limitation.

† You shall speak no word of lack or limitation.

† You shall let go and let God do it.

† You shall deal honorably with God and all human instruments through whom God's good is manifest for you.

† You shall keep your wealth circulating wisely.

† You shall use your wealth spiritually, mentally, physically and materially for good purposes only.

† You shall not seek something for nothing.

† You shall not bear false witness against the source of your wealth.

† You shall not limit yourself by coveting that which is another's.